THE PLA

Mattie Turnbull

Copyright

This paperback edition is self-published 2024 by Martha Turnbull.

Amazon ISBN 9798326178367
Copyright © Mattie Turnbull 2024
Cover Copyright © Joy Dakers 2024

All rights reserved No part of this publication may be reproduced stored in a retrieval system or transmitted in any form or by any means (electronic mechanical photocopying recording or otherwise) without the prior written permission of the publisher except for brief quotations used for promotion or in reviews

The contents of this book are reflective of the time period and may offend the current viewpoint - this is not the intention - the intention is to re-create an accurate representation of the time.

Jasami Acknowledgements

Editors

Liam Ward
Joy Curtis
Erin McEntegart

Cover Designer

Joy Dakers

Disclaimer

This work reflects attitudes, languages and cultural depictions of the time. These are not intended to cause offence, but are meant to authentically relay the historical essence of the time period.

Author Acknowledgements

The author is grateful to her Jasami Publishing & Productions team and, of course, to her sister Catherine Marco (who is none other than the Plain Child) who ensured the legitimacy of the historic events which took place during her 'growing up' and is reflected in this work.

This is also the opportunity to commend husband, Jackie Boy Turnbull, who chuckled each time his reflection was requested. This has resulted in an exciting and meaningful journey for The Plain Child.

Table of Contents

Prologue: 1958	9
Social Divides	10
Culture	16
Holidays	20
Illness and Healthcare	26
The Plain Child Grows Up	29
The Myth of Ordinariness	32
1976	48
The Ups and Downs in a Cuban Casa	59
A Day of Reckoning	73
Wot? No Darts?	75
Casa and Beyond	80
Exiting Cuba	87
Author Notes	101
Photos	102
About the Author	105

Prologue

*1958
The Year of the Plain Child*

The Plain Child was born in very ordinary circumstances in a very ordinary town on a very ordinary day in 1958. There are those, however, who would not view 1958 as a very ordinary year or Glasgow as a very ordinary city.

That was the year in which stars of Manchester United, the glamour football club of England at that time, were killed in a plane crash near Munich, Germany. The whole of football-crazy Britain went into a deep depression. It was the year in which the last person was executed in Scotland: a monster, accused of eight murders, who astounded all by conducting his own defence. In 1958, Scotland's national paper cost two and a half pence and held that price for four years. Some consumer goods were still sold in guineas. Bill Haley and the Comets caused riots in the centre of Glasgow and everyone loved the Queen (well...). This was the hometown of the Plain Child.

Social Divides

The great social divider of exams to determine class level was still in vogue in education- proud Scotland, where those who passed went off to the Senior Secondary School and those who did not pass went to the Junior equivalent. This was an era of great social insensitivity because the results were often announced in class, which gave Seniors the licence to mock the Juniors. If you were lucky enough to go to the Senior Secondary you were assured of a passport to prosperity; if you went to the Junior Secondary you were assured of a place in the shipyards or factories for the boys and just the factories for the girls. Even shorthand typing jobs, which were the reserve of the Junior Secondary curriculum, were scarce. In this system, the fodder for the thriving heavy industries was assured. Fog was still a huge problem in 1950s Britain, but since the Clean Air Act girls' petticoats were no longer black after one day.

Nearly everyone seemed to go to some kind of prayer house in those days and there was a huge divide between Catholics and Protestants. Catholics were given to call their place of worship a chapel and the Prods called their own a church. It seemed to the Plain Child that church was deemed to be a bit more posh. Protestants could not come to grips with the notion of confession and harangued their Catholic counterparts with such statements as: but WE don't need anyone in between us and God— you do; whilst the Catholics argued that the pretentious word choice of church made sense for the Protestants.

The state paid for separate schools and, although the curriculum was identical, the Protestants insisted that their education was superior. When faced with the accusation that separate schools engendered bigotry, a Catholic Archbishop of the day replied that Catholic schools were not the cause of bigotry but rather the result. Sectarian social divides were manifested in rival soccer teams and have endured to this day. Indeed, a common joke in the 21st century is that if one identifies as a 'Prod,' the question in Glasgow can be asked, "What's it like being a ProDestant?" And the safe answer now is, "Anything's alright as long as you don't enjoy it."

In Glasgow at this time most Catholics were not to be found in many of the professions and the small Jewish population was involved in the rag trade. This was to change dramatically by the 1960s when Catholics and Jews, operating on the basis that the enemy of my enemy is my friend, were often found in companies like Shaughnessy, Quigley and Goldberg. The Jewish mob, however, did have a serious foothold in warehousing or, as we know them today, department stores. These huge sprawling stores exploited many working class families with the lure of buy-now-pay three-months-later, and most households had a line for places with conspicuous names like Goldbergs. A classic Glasgow joke of the time was that people used to say to one another, "Do you want to hear a story?" and then they would really enjoy saying, "Well, it's called Goldybergs and the Three Bills."

The more you bought the better your credit. There were several of these places and people had great allegiance to one or the other. Sadly, in some ways, they have all disappeared. One of the nice features of these stores was of course the restaurant where families could dine rather nicely and pay later. The hoi polloi was now the middle class consumer. It was a special thrill for these families since they would have been most reluctant to take many children to real restaurants.

Nearly everyone in Glasgow, in the year the Plain Child was born, lived in a corporation (council/state housing) or factor's house, or privately rented a flat and paid amazingly cheap rents by 21st century standards. This of course did not encourage a high level of home ownership. Hence when one met someone with the temerity to incur a huge mortgage to buy a house this was known as a bought house and a special reverence was reserved for such individuals. Mostly Protestants and priests seemed to be able to live in these bought houses, which seemed totally incongruous at the time. The Plain Child would one day live in very opulent bought houses, but she didn't know it then.

In 1958, huge, sprawling council estates were erected on the edges of the great city of Glasgow and the term used to justify these social disasters was slum clearance—a seemingly fitting name since Glasgow had earned the ignominious fame of having possibly some of the worst slums in Europe. These schemes housed up to forty-thousand people; all flats with no real gardens and no pubs nearby.

For a city like Glasgow to be bereft of pubs was to ask for trouble.

Some schemes became synonymous with anti-social behaviour and the birth of many gangs. One incredible result was a visit to Glasgow by a famous music hall star by the name of Frankie Vaughan who encouraged the youth of one of the bigger schemes to lay down their arms and the newspaper coverage of this amnesty and the pile of weapons deposited on a spare bit of ground will be indelible from many Glaswegians' minds to this day. It created great excitement and mothers and fathers were very grateful to this benefactor from the south. The reality was that it was one of the most patronising acts ever bestowed upon working class people. To this day it is ridiculed mercilessly.

In those days children made much of their own entertainment, although television had found its way into most homes where they were entertained by such banality as Muffin the Mule (a really boring puppet show) and Andy Pandy, whose sexual proclivity had yet to be questioned. Commercial television was just around the corner, and everyone thought that Heinz beans and soup were Scottish products. The Scots were visibly embarrassed by the local efforts of Scottish television which seemed to offer only Gaelic singers which no one understood, and avant-garde plays which portrayed only the miserable side of Glasgow; and this before John Osborne's kitchen sink dramas.

At this time the Scots all understood one another and shared the same humour. Glaswegians didn't really know they had an accent except that all those who appeared on English television seemed to be awfully posh. This was before the advent of the resurgence of Scottish nationalism. Newcastle was, of course, just as deserving of a Frankie Vaughan visit—as were many cities in the UK at this time.

Culture

In 1958, all the men wore black and many wore hats. Nylon coloured shirts were a few years away; as were Chinese restaurants, where one could order a bottle of cheap Spanish Sauterne and be embarrassed to death when the waiter dropped a spot in your glass and no one was game enough to drink the sample. Everyone wanted to throw up after the first taste. Several real restaurants were around in Glasgow in 1958 but the parents and relatives of the Plain Child would have known that they were not for them—far too expensive for the East End of Glasgow punters.

By and large mammies stayed at home and made interesting cakes and visited their pals and pushed babies in wonderful Silver Cross prams. These mammies vied with one another about things like knitted jumpers with amazing cable stitches and white socks. Tea was always ready by five in the afternoon, when everyone seemed to be able to muster a huge appetite for the likes of steak pie, mince and potatoes, or liver and onions. The men poured from the factories to the sound of a horn and meandered their way home in electric tram cars. There were also trolley buses in Glasgow in 1958 and the locals called them silent death, since they used to swoop upon unsuspecting old people as they scampered across busy intersections or moved forward too quickly at the bus stops.

1958 was the period in which Scotland was predominantly white, but this included a smattering of Italian ex-prisoners of war who made good money introducing exotic ice cream parlours and fish and chip shops where one could sit in just like a real restaurant. Mothers used to tell their children stories of Italians who seemed to own all the fish and chip shops, hairdressers and ice cream parlours and, although patronised most days of their lives, Glaswegians felt something about it all.

Because the Italians stayed in Scotland at the end of World War II after changing sides to join the Allies in 1943, the story goes that people used to go to their local fish and chip shop and, instead of asking for threepence worth of chips, they would ask for threepence worth of stab-in-the-back, please. That one always took a trick.

People still made insensitive remarks about the far-flung exotic cultures which the Queen and the Duke of Edinburgh always seemed to be visiting. The Maori of New Zealand and the South African Zulus were of particular attention; and like the baying crowd watching the trapeze artist who might fall any minute, the spears never seemed far away from the sweating royals.

The map of the world was predominantly red the year the Plain Child was born and everyone was awfully proud of this and had no idea of the foment to come in the next decade or two. Lots of mammies and daddies talked of emigrating to places like Australia and Canada and all the children were terrified this might come to pass since it was really cold in Canada and by all accounts really hot in Australia. And anyway, in Australia they didn't have flush toilets—so they heard—and just what that meant the children could not imagine.

Holidays

By and large, annual holidays took the form of a trip of about thirty miles to the Ayrshire coast. Families rented other peoples' houses and children wondered where those people went while they were living in them. Often the houses families rented by the sea were much less comfortable than the homes they had left but mammies and daddies were undaunted, and about two weeks before the actual train trip it would be time for the hamper to be packed and sent off to the seaside house to await the arrival of the city folk. The children therefore had two weeks during which they had to run around in their old clothes since all the good stuff had been painstakingly packed into the hamper. Since most houses in Scotland were relatively small, it was always a puzzle as to where the hampers would be stored at the holiday house. Nevertheless, stored they were, and there was great excitement after two weeks' absence to discover all manner of forgotten treasures in the hamper. These holidays were, amazingly, not very restful for mothers, and fathers to a lesser extent, since it was by and large just a change of sink.

The journey on the train took about one and a half hours at the outset, but it was always the case that when the train had just left Glasgow the children claimed hunger and mothers un-wrapped interesting sandwiches (sangwiches to a Glaswegian), cakes and warm milk immediately. The train journey to the coast, which was anticipated on a yearly basis, would in a short time be an evening trip for the Plain Child, taken in a very-envied brand of internal combustion machine. The Plain Child would know nothing of these things since she was known as a change of life baby and her brothers and sisters were well-grown by the time she came along. But she didn't know that then.

The coastal town where the Plain Child's family spent their annual holiday boasted an open air swimming pool curiously called a bathing lake and where, in temperatures of fifty-odd degrees, old-money young women shivered around the edge in the beauty contests. The children sniggered and the adults mercilessly tore the contestants' features to shreds, claiming that Auntie Joan or Auntie Mary could leave them for dead. Each morning was just like at home, with mother in a strange kitchen, missing all her favourite utensils and cooking her head off. When the brood was ready, the trek to the beach commenced and father made a quick getaway to the local pub for opening time. All pubs were called the Red Lion to save confusion, and after his session he would grace the family on the beach with his presence for half an hour since it was now lunch time.

Sometimes the children were treated to a packed lunch—which always sounded exotic—but the sandwiches were usually dropped and got covered in sand and people were often losing silver money which disappeared incredibly quickly in the dunes. One year, one of the Plain Child's two brothers managed to swallow a huge copper penny which got lodged in his throat. This was a very exciting happening since he had to be turned upside down and punched to kingdom come in order to dislodge it. A ghoulish crowd gathered and cheered the distraught father on and the story is told to this day.

The seaside, or doon the coast, as it was called in those days, had an interesting array of entertainment on the beach, from the Punch and Judy Show to the Salvation Army Band who entreated all to have their cup running over. The puppets of the Punch and Judy Show were very violent, always bashing each other over the head and disappearing behind the curtains, but the children couldn't get enough of this and screamed for more. The Salvation Army were seen as somehow pagan, especially to the Catholics who had the privileged notion that only they would see the kingdom of heaven drilled into them. That is, they knew better since they had been endowed with the faith and by and large should pity the likes of the Sally Ann. Nevertheless, the children seemed to enjoy the songs and the bright uniforms but forgot all about them until they grew old enough to go to pubs where they were asked for money by the same people in uniforms. There were always raging arguments in Glasgow regarding whether or not the Sally Ann practised what they preached since they got their funds in dens of ill repute.

One of the great features of the holiday was always the funfair, but it cost the mothers and fathers an arm and a leg and, when taken there, mothers would always infuriatingly suggest that the children have a wee walk around first. The most exciting roller coasters were, of course, the Big Dipper and the precarious Mouse, which were all the more thrilling for the real possibility that someone may hurtle right over their edge. It never seemed to happen, but it was no less exciting for the anticipation.

The two week holiday for the children was over all too soon and mother was invariably, having done her duty, very glad to get back to her own kitchen and father back to his regular pub. The sun always seemed to be shining on holiday, at least for the children, and the proof of this was that all the ankles were white beneath the sock line. This gave a great measure of pride upon return, especially if pals had not had the privilege of two weeks away.

The school holidays seemed to go on forever and it was so hot — a memory everyone shared from childhood — that the tar definitely melted in the streets. It might have been that the streets of Glasgow used to be paved with low grade tarmac, since it doesn't seem to be a problem today. Places that children played in the year the Plain Child was born were variously known as up the muck or over the loany. These were simply spare bits of ground where children discovered kissing games among other interesting pursuits. Up the muck was exactly as it sounds and today the fields are covered in small efficient factories where the Plain Child's brother was eventually to start a reasonably profitable business making all manner of signs. The Loany was quite different in as much as it was covered in long grass where those same children were often excited by the thought that one of the more adventurous girls would produce what became known as the furry glove. Nobody now remembers her name but the very mention of the furry glove gives rise to all manner of sniggers and secret memories.

Illness and Healthcare

In 1958 Polio was still rampant and children were quietly terrified of the thought of being stuck in an iron lung. Horror stories abounded, particularly of the dangers of catching it at the local swimming baths. For all its poverty, the great British cities all had neighbourhood Victorian edifices which doubled as swimming pools. There didn't seem to be any trainers around to teach children to swim but eventually most seemed to manage some semblance of the crawl, the girls mostly favouring the breaststroke. These were places to show off and to meet one's pals shivering by the side of the water, terrified that the boys would throw the girls in. Many of the boys were terrified too, and on a visit to such a pool many years later there was a real possibility of finding one or two toenails which had been there for the past forty years.

But the greatest social advance in British history, the National Health Service, was safely entrenched by 1958 and people were very proud of this. The system in America was much maligned and there was always much criticism of those Yanks getting false teeth, glasses and having babies at British expense. Doctors were allocated numbers of patients called, for some reason, a panel, and it seemed that waiting rooms were always full, if not overflowing. The strangest thing was that there was never any order when one was waiting one's turn and it became a terribly anxious waiting game trying to figure out who was next. No one ever bothered to ask who came before and the possibility of cheating was ever-present. The receptionists always seemed to be a bit self-righteous and never imparted any clues. No one ever seemed to talk to one another, to share ailments, but mostly it seemed everyone was there with a dreadful hacking cough. Nevertheless, mothers and fathers were awfully proud of the system and shared this pride with one another and reminisced about how dreadful it was before that icon, the National Health Service.

The Plain Child's sister actually had her tonsils out in their own house, which must have been around 1947, and one of the Plain Child's sisters tells a wonderful story of seeing the kitchen table being made ready for the surgeon and being sent to sit outdoors on the coal bunker while the butcher did his work. Since the houses were joined, children from next door joined the sister on the bunker but refused to believe someone's throat was being slit even as they swung their legs. The sister survived and to this day is embarrassed by the thought of such ignominy. A few years later the same sister contracted Scarlet Fever, which was almost as horrific as Polio, but this time an ambulance came and took her to a hospital and she was not to be seen again for three weeks. These were the worst health problems to afflict the Plain Child's family for a long time so they were, by and large, most fortunate.

The Plain Child Grows Up
"Out She Comes!"

Enough of anonymity. Now you are about to know the name of the Plain Child. Not her real name—oh no! But this will do, I think.

When Mary started to become aware of all of her surroundings and also aware of how much her two brothers and sisters enjoyed her, rather than capitalise on this, she somehow understood that she was quite privileged. That is, by the time she was five years old, the world was awash with change and excitement. The Beatles burst onto the scene, snatching the rock and crooner thrones from such as Gene Vincent, Bill Haley, Frank Sinatra and even Elvis Presley! Grist to the mill of Mary's birth year is that Elvis was granted an extension to his national service (he went to Germany) from late 1957 to 1958. It was a very good year.

From 1963, nothing would ever be the same, and Mary was a great beneficiary of these changes, both social and political. The emergence of the great Second Wave of Feminism resulted in Mary's opportunities being almost unlimited. Notably, she still could not become a Catholic Priest. Nevertheless, she did follow the pattern of her older sisters' education and attended an all girls high school. By this time however, the students were allowed to wear some reasonable attire—not the prescriptive gym-slip of old. She emerged well-qualified and should have been ready for the world ahead.

However, throughout Mary's childhood days, from her First Communion/Confirmation to her now comprehensive schooling—no more Senior or Junior stuff—she remained convinced that she was plain, despite others acclaiming her enormous appeal in all manner of ways. This was evidenced by the pals of the others in the family as well as the extended family, who would remark that she was a wee smasher, or would say: see her and that Badminton; or, she's amazing and she's a really nice wee lassie.

Perhaps due to her notion of her ordinariness, human nature being what it is, she became one of the best badminton players of her time. She was just a natural athlete and, in a more equal, progressive time, she would no doubt have served her country.

Suffice to say, she was lauded by her contemporaries, many of whom were boys!

Around this time, she gained a place at uni, which her father—a Red Clyde Communist—rejoiced in. One of his most serious resolutions was that of high-quality political and contemporary education for all. The Plain Child fulfilled his aspirations when she was eighteen, the year he died. Years later she found his passion for education detailed in a letter he had written and never sent. The self-proclaimed Plain Child was on her way with the added satisfaction that her father's chest would have expanded so far with pride that he would not have been left with a button on his jacket.

However, university was not for the emerging, multifaceted Mary, as she began to appreciate the world's opportunities in a less structured learning process, but she still clung to the notion that, apart from her sporting prowess, she will still be pretty ordinary.

The Myth of Ordinariness

Contemporary times have created this myth of ordinariness that has been referenced throughout history. Mary felt she suffered from this ordinariness that others had suffered from before.

Isla, Todd, Margaret, and Andy had been meeting every third Thursday of the month for almost as long as they could remember; but in reality it had been for nine years. The records proved it. Although there were no formal arrangements for their meetings, due to Margaret's employment as a Hansard reporter for the State Parliament, she felt compelled to give order to their not-so-avid but, as they saw it, interesting deliberations. Because they were all modest and ordinary mortals, they called their third Thursday of the month meetings the Family Conversation. Margaret had never really liked that label—especially since she had assumed the role of Secretary—and had several suggestions of her own. However, she kept these to herself in order to fulfil their agenda without rancour of any kind.

They were all family. Todd and Andy were brothers, and Isla and Margaret were their spouses respectively. The history of their less ordinary denouement erupted subsequent to one particular event in Andy's life. This event had a particularly profound effect on the conduct of their—as deemed by themselves—ordinary lives. It is important for the reader to anticipate that this event caused the demise of not only their monthly meetings, but also their relationships, which ceased to exist after the event.

At the time the Family Conversation was established, Isla and Todd and Margaret and Andy were all very busy seeing their older children off into the world and were looking forward to the empty nest stage of their lives as soon as the late babies were grown. Neither couple had any particular inclination at that time to have a formal relationship with the other.

To date, they had shared birthdays and Christmas and sometimes they enjoyed a cheap and cheerful meal in each other's suburbs. However, their relationships became more formal under the auspices of the Family Conversation. As their routine became entrenched, although none had any real notion of the importance of the art of philosophising, they all secretly believed that their thoughts and quiet opinions at the Thursday meetings were undeniably of a higher order. This was because they deemed themselves to be ordinary or normal punters. It was not usual for ordinary or normal punters to state a strong opinion on a subject lest they be seen as a show off.

This, of course, was before Andy's unordinary event.

In due course Margaret persuaded the others to move their Family Conversation to a more profound basis, no doubt due to her ascendancy in the readings of the great philosophers. Each of them was willing if not necessarily enthusiastic, but made the commitment without demur. The venue remained the same and the new approach entailed a new level of solemnity—just like a book club really. Cheese and biscuits and olives were on offer, sometimes even an exotic pâté. This is quite ordinary fare for the ordinary. Beer and wine too were requisite as they settled down for their new approach to conversation on the third Thursday of each month.

They had decided that they would favour one particular topic each Thursday. For example, one evening might be devoted to discussing capital punishment, another to climate change, another to the current social mores—which were, of course, quite different from their own upbringing. Although these topics were all philosophical by definition, this did not appear to encourage Margaret or Andy to pursue this notion at that time.

The little meetings were, by and large, benign, eliciting little passion. Of course, several issues were off limits: politics and religion being the two excluded from the agenda, but they all secretly wished they were on the agenda because they would have generated at least a little passion. But each was afraid that if these types of complex, far-reaching outings were allowed, they ran the risk of thought-exposure, which could result in a fracas of unknown proportions. So, on and on went the Family Conversation meetings for nine years. If truth be known they were all really bored with the whole thing, but they acknowledged that this veneer of ordinariness was essential to their somewhat clandestine hopes and desires.

At this particular time Margaret had a pal who was at the same empty nest stage of her life whose name was Morag. Morag was a teacher at a private school and she taught religious doctrine. Margaret was a bit suspicious about religious doctrine or indeed religious anything, but Morag was very confident and influential in Margaret's life because both their sons played for the same football team— not soccer (since they all hailed from Scotland)— and they were always in attendance to encourage their boys in any way, shape or form. Sometimes the boys were embarrassed by their enthusiasm and told their mums so, but the mums were undaunted and saw their support as a necessary role in the development of their children.

Morag is important to this story only because she was the conduit for Margaret's later development into a more academic life, similar to the one that she herself enjoyed. However, if Margaret had been so inclined, she could have invited Morag to share some of her experiences in her everyday life at the Parliament. Now there was a learning curve for the most and the least important of the population; but of course Morag would not, at that time, have understood the importance of the ability to write shorthand—Pitmans to boot. In Morag's high school days, shorthand was for those who did not quite make the grade academically. Shorthand, Pitman's of course, would get one a job alright, but not one with quite the same status as a teacher.

Margaret was therefore grateful to Morag when she suggested they do a night class in Philosophy. In order not to embarrass her teacher pal, Margaret got herself a little book called Introduction to Philosophy. Andy nearly went mad because, in anticipation of Margaret's class attendance, she devoured every page. No meals were cooked, no house was cleaned, no social arrangements were made, and she even resisted attendance at her son's football games. However, dear reader, this was not the event which resulted in the dis-establishment of the Family Conversation.

Andy was a plumber who earned a seriously good living, as all plumbers do. But he was used to order in his domestic life and became really concerned by this philosophical influence. A strange thing happened when Margaret started her Tuesday night philosophy class. It was fortunate that it was held on a Tuesday night because her son's football games were on a Wednesday, which meant that she was able to resume her interest in her son's potential

World Cup endeavours as well as resuming some of the household chores; only some, because she never, ever made the beds again.

The strange thing that happened was that, unbeknown to Margaret, while she was at her classes, Andy himself was drawn to her little book on philosophy. Although he understood he was just a plumber and a novice and that was a very ordinary place to be, each week he got more and more excited about Kierkegaard's ideas—especially his take on the religious sphere. As a simple chap, Andy had always thought that to believe some of the stuff about God and Christian faith (he had been reared a 24 carat Catholic) was a bit of an ask, and low and behold this was what Kierkegaard believed too. What a coup! He was loath to discuss his enlightenment with Margaret, who was now full-bottle on the lot of them, her current favourite being Simone de Beauvoir. Since Andy thought that Simone de Beauvoir was a man, he understood little of his good wife's language when quoting her heroine.

So, these were the beginnings of Margaret and Andy's sortie into higher learning, although they still talked of themselves as just ordinary and didn't really share much of their new-found illumination.

Although there was limited cross-fertilisation between Margaret and Andy about their new-found philosophy scholarship, both now had a great and profound understanding of the cause of reason in the face of the irrationality and superstition associated with their own rearing. Despite this, they did not share this in any meaningful way, which was a great pity because they were both infused with the complexity of human behaviour—in particular the moral compass and values. Due to this reluctance to share, or indeed expound, their findings and thoughts to each other, neither knew they were both extremely interested in Jung and Freud's ideas on sexuality and sexual proclivity. They were both afraid to discuss their findings due to the other's potential scorn. They were obviously just a tad afraid to lose their ordinariness.

In the meantime Todd and Isla appeared to be fulfilled in their suburban lives. But Todd was actually a frustrated tree lopper and did not earn a seriously good living like his brother Andy. Todd and Isla however had a lovely home which Margaret and Andy secretly discussed. What they discussed was that they couldn't really figure out how they could afford all the trappings of their less ordinary home since Isla, at this time, did not sell her labour on the market.

Isla, meanwhile, was finding herself like her brother and sister-in-law. Not for her football watching from the lines; no, Isla was on a different trajectory. Since her childhood, she had always adored Brigitte Bardot and aspired to replicate her. This she kept a secret from the electrician, who favoured more of the James Bond stuff, and he, in turn, kept this a secret from Isla. She loved to hear Brigitte speak in French, which she thought was just the sexiest thing; but of course she didn't understand a word.

As chance would have it, one day while at the local shopping centre, when she was looking for a gift for her best pal Flora, she tripped on a discarded ice cream stick and down she went. Isla deemed herself to be very ordinary and never drew attention to herself in any way, shape or form, which only made the fall all the more excruciating. It wasn't really the pain or the fact that her skirt was now around her waist, it was the humiliation and the attention she had garnered as a result. She quite honestly thought that if she tried to get up, she might slip again, because it was quite a large ice cream on a stick—chocolate too.

At that particular moment the Frenchman Monsieur Flaubert had to pass the very spot Isla had conducted her embarrassing escapade, this being on his way to the cigar chop. This was the only remaining cigar shop in the country so it was very important to people who still chomped. He was therefore proceeding with great haste when he came upon Isla. Unlike several passing shoppers who were rather enjoying the spectacle, Monsieur Flaubert quickly picked her up with great aplomb (as only the French can) and escorted her to the cigar shop. She was so grateful that she resisted giving him a lecture about the dangers of smoking. She also resisted because he was pretty specky-looking and just about the same age and stage she was. After he had purchased his evil weeds, he suggested a café au lait and—not necessarily because he was French, but a little bit because he was French—she accepted with alacrity. Because she was so ordinary she didn't understand this expression, but was inclined to say yes to whatever his pursuit might be.

The rest is possibly predictable but worth telling. Isla fell truly, madly, deeply, in love with Monsieur Flaubert and, from that day on, they regularly met outside the cigar shop. He taught her French beyond simply café au lait. Sometimes he called her Brigitte, which curled her toes, and they loved each other from that first day they met. The electrician knew nought of this of course. Once in a while Isla slipped up and said merci instead of thanks, or even started a sentence with the bon mots voulez-vous.... when she was simply enquiring if he would like a cup of tea. Naturally, she felt a bit less ordinary from that point on.

The story of Todd is not quite as romantic as that of his wife Isla. His was more a story of Breakin' Bad due to his desire to impress others with his lovely home and gardens but he had run up massive debts. He was therefore on constant alert should something drop in his mailbox with the official sender's moniker plastered all over the envelope. Should Isla have got to them first, there was no limit in his mind as to what might ensue. He, of course, got himself a Post Office box that he could monitor a lot easier than she could.

Around the same time as Isla had had her fall, Todd was tree-lopping at a garden in a very affluent suburb. The owner—a French chap (Todd like many others was not overly fond of the Frogs)—engaged him in a conversation. The conversation eventually got around to how hard it was for Todd to make enough money to support his lifestyle and to keep up appearances. Albeit, as he explained, in comparison with the French guy's opulence Todd's environs were pretty ordinary.

As luck would have it, the French guy whose name was, coincidentally, Monsieur Flaubert, suggested that if Todd had the time or inclination to do a bit of running for him he would never have to worry again about maintaining his lifestyle. Nothing would be in writing of course: it would simply be a pickup and drop off once a week to some addresses in Monsieur Flaubert's neighbourhood. This was an offer too hard to resist and the deal was struck. Naturally, this deal was too good to be true and came to a sticky end for Todd.

On one of the days after the pick up from Monsieur Flaubert, he had a huge fall from one of those Marlock Gum trees and he broke one of his legs. After getting plastered up and feeling a bit traumatised, he remembered he had missed the delivery. What's more, as he was paid piece rates, there would be no money for a few weeks. He was distraught. Worst of all, he did not have a contact telephone number to advise his paymaster of his misfortune.

As we now know, Monsieur Flaubert frequented the cigar store (the only one left in the country). Todd knew this too as it had come up in a conversation at pick up times. He also knew that the visit to the Cigar Store—usually at a certain time on a certain day—was within the specified hour. So he thought it would be an opportunity to advise the Monsieur of his misfortune regarding the tree episode and to offload the stash in the meantime. Isla was happy to transport Todd to the shopping centre, where she dropped him off while she purportedly did a little shopping. She of course had no idea that they might both rendezvous with Monsieur Flaubert. As Todd approached the cigar shop, he was conscious of someone following him at a pace: casual, but with obvious impetus. The rest is history. He was arrested on possession of drugs and marched off to wherever people are marched off to in these circumstances. Breakin' Bad did not pay Todd very well at all. Meanwhile, Isla and Todd were continuing along in their comfortable way (well, it looked that way to Margaret and Andy and vice versa) and maintained their position of ordinary, which suited all of them.

It had happened like this: Andy had a job to do in the very shopping centre where Isla had met Monsieur Flaubert those few years previously. Andy and Todd had no idea that each was in the vicinity of the other and Monsieur Flaubert had just arrived at the cigar shop and would later fulfil his mission to rendezvous with Isla. Andy was outside the cigar shop attending to the various small pipes that only a plumber would understand when he and Monsieur Flaubert became conscious of each other.

The eyes of Andy and Flaubert met and that was it. They embraced each other and made their way out of the centre arm in arm. Isla witnessed this with incredulity, as did Todd, who was in the process of being handcuffed. Something told him it was more than coincidence that she happened to be in the doorway of a cigar shop given that she had never smoked anything in her life. He was also able to discern something more than surprise in her reaction to the event. She subsequently collapsed, calling out to her departing lover, "Please Monsieur, don't leave me here. Je t'aime!." Todd, wringing his cuffed hands, was transfixed by what he had witnessed; but the facts were there. He and Isla could never reconcile. He knew this and was devastated.

Isla was privy to all these revelations and then also knew there was no hope of reconciliation. Not only was she devastated at the loss of Monsieur Flaubert, she now understood that Todd had, for whatever reason, withheld something very important from her. She acknowledged that it would take a long time to try to understand what had happened. Neither would recover.

By contrast to the others, Margaret, due to her now well-developed understanding of the great philosophers, was able to somehow come to terms with all that had gone before them on this fateful day. She obviously banished Andy immediately, retreated for a while, and considered her future.

She discussed it all with her friend Margot who had now recognised that Margaret was no ordinary individual. She had unlimited potential in so many spheres. She had resourcefulness like no other and Andy had been more than generous to her financially. She was an independent woman. She was now a latter-day Simone de Beauvoir, except that if she was to write about women today she would refuse to be labelled as other. She could now secure her own destiny.

Her own destiny was that she became the most widely-read feminist author in the English speaking world (she also had left-leaning tendencies which had emerged slowly in her literature). She was feted wherever she went. She chose her friends carefully and refused to be drawn on her own experience. However, it was obvious that her first great novel was in fact autobiographical, replete with a few teaspoonfuls of spice.

Despite everything, she was very grateful for the nine years of ordinariness afforded by Andy and Isla and Todd, but concluded that it was in the beginning of the tenth year of the Family Conversation, when the ordinary became extraordinary and the lives of these four ordinary people were quietly and secretly changed, that the mystery of ordinariness had been solved. There is no such thing as ordinariness. It was just that Andy's event topped the lot.

1976
The Beginning of the End of the Plain Child

Now it's 1976, the Plain Child has given in and reluctantly accepted that she is no longer a plain person. Why? Because she was much sought after by both genders alike. Having given up the notion of the formality of a tertiary education, she and one of her best pals (of like-mind) embarked on a few years of blissful youth. Her best pal is called Angela and they sold their labour to various institutions of leisure, such as Butlins' Holiday Camps, pubs in the Scottish Highlands and Islands and, woe-betide-them, to the fleshpots of places such as Aberdeen and Frome in Somerset. They also chose to 'ave a laugh in big laundries situated in Liverpool, Manchester and even London.

Indeed, nothing was beyond the pair and their crowning glory was that they spent a dodgy year in Eastern Europe as 'New Age Travellers.' Suffice to say that they both fell in love with the same Serbian/Croatian called Darkan but resolved the matter by moving on and reading a good book.

Their skirmishes have no place in this book but, perhaps in due course, a sequel!

1977: The Year That Shook Their World

With these experiences under their belts, the epitome of this period naturally lent itself to the United States of America. Not for them, however; the tried and true of the established destinations was too ordinary now and their quest was for something completely different.

Their agreed destination was a quaint little town on the south-west coast of Florida, called Flamingo, where they thought they might start a little business. Perhaps a restaurant specialising in Haggis with a Latin American flavour or a more down to earth house-cleaning business to cater for retirees or Snowbirds, as they are colloquially known, for flying down to warm-weather states in the winter. They believed that their experiences would serve them well. But this was not to be.

It was a glorious spring—April to be precise— and certainly warmer than the Scottish spring they had just departed from. Passports in hand, they boarded a flight from Miami which they thought was bound for Key West (which would've been the conduit to Flamingo); but on surveying the passengers, they were dismayed to see that they were all wearing US military uniforms and were whispering the word contraband to each other as the flight took off. They didn't speak to each other for a bit but then realised that their original flight would possibly take less than an hour—in fact on a good day probably no more than forty minutes! So, three hours later, what happened? Mary and Angela had no idea they were accidentally bound for Havana in Cuba. In April 1977, it was one of the last redoubts of the Russian Communist era, only twelve years away from the wall coming down.

Well, as it happens, they arrived in Cuba through the means of several crazy bungles along the way. The first was that they were allowed on the plane. They did not bother to inquire regarding this slip-up because by this time, due to their snooping on the conversations taking place along the aisles, it was not difficult to conclude their fate and the fate of the American service people on the plane. They rationalised that they did have the political blunders up their sleeves which would enable them to consult with one of the more sympathetic women on the flight. When put sagely to this officer, she confirmed that, although 1977 was the year in which Cuba and the US were beginning to test the waters of rapprochement, unfortunately the Cubans would still need good reason to allow two lassies from the East End of Glasgow to enter their hallowed Communist ground. Bear in mind they did not have a visa, a hotel room or indeed any good reason to be alighting in Cuba. The charming officer listened carefully to their story and offered a quick solution: they were to be US scholarship students to the University of Havana which was established in 1728 and supported by the American Government. This win-win solution was a brainchild. The paperwork was hastily assembled, authorised, photocopied (yes there was a printer on this plane in 1977) and safely stored in their hand luggage, which wasn't conspicuous at all—indeed totally appropriate for a uni student of this period.

Mary and Angela were also given many US dollars in exchange for their silence and since there was not much indulgence to buy in Cuba in 1977, they were ecstatic and could not conceal their giggles of excitement at this chain of events. Interestingly, the university offered courses in: politics, Afro-Caribbean studies, music, literature, philosophy, sociology, history, biology and international relations. Mary and Angela could not believe their luck since they both claimed to be heavily interested in all of these disciplines. Mary opted for Afro-Caribbean Studies and Angela opted for biology and smiled conspiratorially at each other as they signed the paperwork, wondering where these disciplines could take them in the future. The language of study was Spanish, but intensive Spanish language lessons were included in their secret pact with the US military establishment.

Naturally, they were reluctant to tell their family and friends of their misadventure, so they settled on advising them that they 'were somewhere in South Florida' and were employed as teachers of English as a second language. This advice naturally puzzled the receivers of this information, since, just like the Glaswegians, the Americans did indeed have English as their first language; but given the level of independence of young people of the era, the odd postcard sufficed to confirm their safety to their families.

They disembarked from the plane at Guantanamo Bay Naval Base and were taken to the Cuban/USA border where they were treated with the utmost respect. They passed through the border without incident and their next mode of transport was a 1959 Chevrolet, with the top down, which was to taxi them to the university campus where their accommodation was. However, they had no idea that it was more than five hundred miles from the US naval base! Of course they stopped from time to time but this was no great comfort to them during their thirteen-hour ride since they genuinely had no idea where they were and no maps of the island state were available. On reflection, they remembered that five hundred miles would have taken them from Glasgow to Aberdeen four times and this gave them some comfort, daft as it sounded later from a distance.

Mary turned to Angela as they swept along the dusty 1977 roads, noting the many farms—but not many people—and Mary whispered in her best non-intelligible Glasgow accent, "Aw shit, this is not as romantic as we thought it might be. 'Ave you got any back up plan?" To which Angela replied "Aye ma heid." At this they both managed a grimace, but after their first stop at the most interesting little restaurant in Camaguey, they were so enchanted that they forgot all concern. Their next two stops were Sancti Spiritus and Cienfuegos, which were equally charming. As they approached Havana, Angela remarked "I cannot believe we have been so amazingly lucky to be the beneficiaries of the US's mistake of landing us here," to which Mary astutely replied, "This is just the beginning. I think we are about to meet our grand passions in this place." Little did they know that there would be the later world-wide phenomenon of the incarceration of prisoners from all over the world in this place.

They arrived at the University of Havana and approached their potential accommodation, which was a huge recently built house where they could share a room and be provided with two meals a day. If this accommodation was satisfactory for them, it would entail a twenty-five minute stroll (always in a clement climate) to the campus. So, on the face of it, all seemed ideal. They were invited to stay at least a couple of nights to decide whether or not they would accept this arrangement or whether they would seek to find a room in a Cuba Casa, which would ensure getting to know the locals, as it was among other attractions offered by the city centre of such a legendary locale as Havana (HaBana).

This confirmed for them that the structures of Communism were indeed largely propagandised by the West. Their potential level of comfort in this exotic destination was not troubling for them. They were really well-read and had lots of experience of other cultures—remember, they hailed from an increasingly multicultural Glasgow (to be City of Culture in 1988)—and from their experience in those towns south of the border, as well as exotic destinations in Eastern Europe in the early 1970s, they were undaunted. They understood only too well the privations which they might encounter, but also due to their philosophical 'left' political persuasion, rather than be afraid, they were intrigued to see how it all worked. Their Eastern European experience would serve them well to an extent, but nothing prepared them for the excitement of their time in Castro's Cuba. Among other things, like cigars and tango music, they could not wait to visit the Bay of Pigs—not that they thought for a moment there would have been any pigs there, but then they conceded that you never know. As it happens, they were right, because the bay appears to have been named for a trigger fish that is common to the bay, and the Spanish name for that fish is close to the Spanish name for pigs. So the English translation comes out as 'pigs.'

Nevertheless, they were together through thick and thin during their year sojourn 'at uni yooni' in this part of the world, which was only 90 miles from the US Florida peninsula, and, although officially being declared independent in 1902, was still heavily influenced by the Unites States of America until 1959.

Cuban Politics from then until now.

Cuba has five universities: the University of Havana (founded 1728), Oriente University at Santiago de Cuba (1947), the University of Las Villas at Santa Clara (1952), University of Camagüey (1974), and the University of Pinar Del-Rio. Workers' improvement courses (superación obrera), to raise adults to the sixth-grade level, and technical training schools (mínimo técnico), to develop unskilled workers' potentials and retrain other workers for new jobs, were instituted after 1961. Special worker-farmer schools prepared workers and peasants for enrolment at the universities and for skilled positions in industrial and agricultural enterprises. In 2003, about 34% of the tertiary age population were enrolled in some type of higher education program. The adult literacy rate in 2004 was estimated at about 99.8%. So at least our new students knew that nearly 100% of Cubans could read and write Spanish!

Cuba's coming of age in 1959, and the copious amounts of support it received from the Soviet Union, was in some ways disrupted by a movement —some called it 'colonial'—of Cuban military troops to Angola in West Africa; which had achieved independence from Portugal in 1975 and was experiencing a Marxist thrust for political control which Cuba supported. The Cuban presence in Angola ceased only in 1991, which meant that the Cuba that Mary and Angela were immersed in was ironically a Cuba that had now embarked on the path of serious political sway in Angola, which was similar to the control that the USA had retained for many years over Cuba. But, of course, Cuba's access to Angola's oil reserves ceased in 1988, as did the Soviet Union's assistance due to this the following year. This was a heady time for Cuba and the unintended travellers. (Cuba a History: 2010) [1]

So the Cuba that Mary and Angela arrived in was a Cuba that still bore the hallmarks of its political history. Coming from the west, they were somewhat enchanted by what they encountered: a population of eleven and a half million people—

twice the size of Scotland, but only twenty-thousand square kilometres larger, which gave their new home a much higher density. They encountered a country which ensured its population had a monthly ration of staples, free medicine for all and free education from the age of five through university.

They also acknowledged, again, some of the place's history. In particular Cuba's approach to the medical profession was noted to be 'the envy of the world,' as the Cuban health system is recognised worldwide for its excellence and its efficiency. Despite extremely limited resources and the dramatic impact caused by the economic sanctions imposed by the United States for more than half a century, Cuba had managed to guarantee access to care for all segments of the population and obtain results similar to those of the most developed nations.

Although, at the time, Mary and Angela were not aware of the movement to normalise relations between the US and Cuba during the Carter administration (1977 – 1981), what they found was civilised and perfect for their adventures. After all, Mary and Angela thought that nineteen was a civilised age to be.

The Ups and Downs in a Cuban Casa

As Mary and Angela checked in to their new and completely unexpected chapter of their lives at their University of Havana, they discovered, much to their chagrin, that the reality of the accommodation offered at their university did not appeal. They deemed themselves to be more mature than their potential co-students. Therefore, the decision was made that they would seek Casa accommodation. However, Mary was particularly nervous of this as she was unfamiliar with the area, stating, "It's one thing to sleep in an apartment in Sofia and earn a quid picking grapes, but it doesn't look very civilised here, Ange," to which Angela replied, "Aye, but this is Cuba and the music will be better."

Mary's concerns were immediately assuaged and with the courtesy of yet another trip in a vintage car —this time a 1958 Studebaker, which was not nearly as flash as the one they had arrived in—they were deposited in the centre of Havana. Fortunately, they didn't have to worry too much about money because of their fortuitous escapade in the US

Military plane and resulting payoff, so began to be rather generous with their tipping. The Cubans did not appear to know much about Scotland and its reputation for thrift, which they decided was a pity since their generosity could have boosted Scottish tourism.

Although they had done some research into the notion of sharing with a family and agreed that this seemed like a sensible and exciting option, the reality was somewhat different. They had only three or four days to secure an accommodation scenario which would be appropriate for their needs. As they strolled the busy streets of Havana, they were both quiet for a bit as they took in the street scenes in all their vibrance. Since it was still light as they commenced their research and indeed search, they became aware that there were hardly any street trees but there were very narrow pavements. Given that so many of the cars were not only amazingly long but also very wide, this didn't surprise them, although the cars themselves did. As they took account of many other visuals—basking in the perfect temperature: twenty-eight degrees celsius or seventy-eight degrees in old-money fahrenheit—which included lots of pubs, they noted that Johnny Walker and other Scotch whiskies were on sale all over the place. Mary made the observation: "It's amazing that a wee country like Scotland can be represented to this extent all over the world," and of course Angela nodded in proud agreement. They had of course for the moment forgotten that rum's presence was also ubiquitous in the First World!

The high incidence of graffiti assaulted them and the duo questioned whether this could be deemed to be art? They would discuss this later at length when they met many artists in the various exciting pubs in the city centre. What sort of looked like graffiti was in fact many, many portrayals of sporting and political heroes. Whilst they were aware of the political identities like Fidel Castro and Che Guevara, their knowledge of basketball was akin to their knowledge of Chinese Emperors!

Years later, Mary and Angela began to realise just what effect their time in Cuba had upon their later life and indeed their view of the contemporary world. In due course, they came to love the game, and since many American teams came regularly to compete against the smaller Cubans, there was a wonderful element of divided loyalty and angst. In other words, eventually it came down to which of the boys was more attractive—the rules they never really understood.

They couldn't quite figure out how it was that in these times of the US/Cuba 'cold war' the US basketball exchange was able to continue. They were also quite astonished—although they berated themselves for this—that Cuba actually hosted the World Youth Festival, held in Havana in 1977 for 'Anti-imperialist Solidarity, Peace and Friendship.' But, of course, the actual event took place later in the year when they had become familiar with many of the eccentricities of life in this Communist outpost.

The Influence of Sport
(always more popular than politics)

What a year to be in Cuba! The pair informed themselves that in the spring of 1977, six of the best basketball players from across the United States, alongside five others from South Dakota State University, flew to Cuba on a DC-9 chartered by Senator Jim Abourezk. Mary chuckled to Angela that a name like Abourezk 'could easily be Russian,' to which Angela promptly replied to her bestie that, "The Ruskies are everywhere. You should know that from our time in Bulgaria and Romania. It was like no other nationality seemed to be around." Mary was suitably chastened, but vowed in her indignant head to contradict her best pal with some well-referenced source. Still, as the records indicated, Russian surname or not, Mr Abourezk had already been to Cuba, as had Senator George McGovern. Both men claimed to be on good terms with Cuban President Fidel Castro, and McGovern was also on the "basketball diplomacy" trip.

As there was no world wide web, their research was old newspapers, which held the best source of information they could access—although they were naturally not as objective as one might have hoped. They showed that Abourezk also claimed that Castro had often given speeches which lasted for at least six hours and that he was a very smart guy. Apparently, the two South Dakota senators hoped the trip, which had the blessing of President Jimmy Carter's administration, would help thaw relations between the two countries.

Boring but important: Senator Abourezk (not Russian at all but, rather, the first Greek Orthodox Christian of Lebanese-Antiochene: Turkish) descent to serve in the United States Senate, recalled that they sold tickets to people who wanted to go on the trip—a rare opportunity for Americans to visit Cuba. "We filled it up easily," he said.

The team stayed at the Marazul Hotel on the ocean in Santa Maria Del Mar. During a welcome banquet hosted by the Cuban Sports Ministry, Abourezk joked that it was the largest group of Americans in Cuba since the botched Bay of Pigs invasion. In two games, the Cuban all-star team had its way with the South Dakota college kids, winning the first game with 91-72 and the second with 88-69. It helped that the Cuban team included members of its 1976 Olympic team.

The trip lasted five days, but there was a home leg later that year. Following the trip, the Cuban national team toured the United States that autumn, as recalled by Charles Lein, who was president of USD (University of South Dakota) from 1977 to 1982. The tour started with Marquette, the 1977 national champions, and included games at USD (University of South Dakota) and SDSU (South Dakota State University), as well as UCLA (University of California Los Angeles).

"It was absolutely unheard of to play Cuba or for Cuba to play anybody in the states," recalled Charles Lein, who was president of USD from 1977 to 1982. It was historic, he added. Apparently the Cubans were older than the college students they played with. Lein lamented that they were physically imposing and stereotypically looked like a bunch of communist goons. They were not friendly. Angela and Mary suggested to each other that perhaps Lein wasn't very friendly either and just a tad judgemental. "Politicians are all the same: self-satisfied and self-righteous," said Mary prophetically. But it was all part of their Cuban baptism!

Although Mary and Angela were indeed excited to realise the zeitgeist of Cuba in 1977, they also acknowledged the 1977 they had left in the UK and indeed Europe. It was the era of the Sloane Ranger and much, much more. But they did test each other about events over there which had been prominent until August 1977, and these included: the first Brit Music Awards, the last natural Smallpox case, Marc Bolan dying in car crash, Red Rum winning the national for the third time, Sex Pistols releasing Never Mind the Bollocks, Silver Jubilee celebrations,

Star Wars opens, and Wade winning Jubilee Wimbledon.

They concluded that the only events which were of any great interest to them were the Star Wars debut, the last natural Smallpox incidence and, on June 4 1977, the damage caused by fans who dug up the pitch at Wembley after Scotland defeated England 2-1, estimated to cost £15,000.

Mary intoned, "I don't have any problem with my national pride thing, cause we don't often beat them and so we have few moments of glory." Angela sagely replied, "But I don't think you remember I was born in Northern Ireland, in Belfast." To which Mary impatiently replied, "It's the same bloody thing. You need to get over that. Scotland's too small for every person who would have liked to have been born there. But while we're here don't complicate things when the Cubans think you're Scottish. Nobody here will know much about Northern Ireland cause it's too Proddy. They're only interested in the Papist stuff here, if they're allowed." Anglela was suitably mollified, whilst not quite understanding what the issue was all about. After all, she was basically a wee Papist by birth. She also knew that the statistics in Scotland at that time certainly favoured a non-Catholic majority!

Criteria for digs

However, Mary and Angela's quest was not to reason why; their mission was to find a decent place to live for the next few years. This mission naturally led to the pub scene where, at their tender age, they agreed that these were the places to locate and confirm solid recommendations for their needs.

Happily, they strolled along the welcoming street and, in due course, came upon a pub which appeared to fit the bill. It was rather boringly named Casa del Mar, at which they nudged each other tellingly at the suggestion that this name had been unadulteratedly plagiarised from the contemporary British love of such exotic locations as Costa del Sol. They thought it was a bit corny. On the other hand they did reflect enough to concede that perhaps the British stole it from Cuba? Anyway, this was the pub they chose on this fateful night and indeed this choice eventuated as their most profound epiphany to date.

They had taken a few moments—but only a few since youthful life has always been hurried— to establish several requirements of their domestic arrangements in Cuba. These included a room each but happy to share a bathroom. Out of their many other daft concessions, this turned out to be one of the daftest. They had realised that many home stays included meals and so they included this in their list. They did NOT want a curfew and did not want any responsibilities with regard to the family with whom they would board. In other words, they wanted to be left alone—not as was often quoted to have been said by Greta Garbo that they wanted to be alone.

Naturally, they both ordered a scotch and soda (although both really preferred a Cuba Libre, the origin of which bears no semblance of connection to rum and coke.) They had agreed to order these drinks so that the locals would note they were not Cuban and that they would therefore receive the requisite attention. Within minutes, several gorgeous guys crossed the crowded room to ask if they could help in any way since they were obviously strangers to their culture. Mary and Angela had anticipated this and had their responses at the ready. When the first guy said sweetly "Jo soy un hombre sincero," they both burst out laughing and responded with, "We're simple women too but not that simple."

However, would you believe, both Carlos and Pablo turned out to be the best thing to have happened to them in the last twenty-four hours. How lucky were they? It turned out that Carlos and Pablo were actually brothers from quite an eminent military family. They were on leave from Angola and had just arrived back twenty-four hours ago. They were in this not-too-classy pub because they could walk and didn't have to drive one of those amazing American convertible monstrosities. This was of course delivered totally tongue in cheek, since most Cubans silently adored the fact that those fabulous automobiles were so manically sought after by the rest of the world, beginning in 1959.

Serendipitously, it turned out that there were two other brothers in the family who had now embarked on their duty in Angola; ergo there were two rooms in some of the most eloquent of homes, in the centre of Havana, which would be perfect for Mary and Angela's aspirations.

So two best pals, aged nineteen, both with a decent exposure to the world of Europe—in particular Eastern Europe—now found themselves in a very foreign place indeed and, although they had experience of many different cultures and male behaviours, none of these had been of a Latin hue; therefore they both indicated to each other their secret trademark of caution. This was represented by a quick flick to the right of their voluminous locks which by and large had never been commented upon before. Alas, this was not to be the case for their Cuban suitors, who smiled knowingly at each other and suggested that Mary looked like Goldie Hawn in Shampoo and Angela looked like Katherine Ross in the movie Stepford Wives. The boys conveyed this in rather charming English, within which they could somehow not avoid pronouncing the letter C as TH.

Of course the girls were flattered, since those movies launched the careers of two very beautiful women. On the other hand, they had to devise a plan to keep things at a more formal level since essentially they needed to find an accommodation commensurate with their needs. Unfortunately, they had not really developed their plan as they had thought they would not need it for another couple of days.

After a quick visit to the Senoras—which is where most of the women of the world make important decisions—Mary and Angela took the bull by the proverbial horns and asked the military chaps if their parents wished to rent the rooms vacated by their brothers and this was met with a resounding yes. Just as an aside, these clever girls had wondered what the sign above the letter A was and, for some reason, they remembered tilde, which kind of added to their interesting scenario. They chuckled as they returned to their new found pals, both thinking that there must be slang in Glasgow for the word tilde, and could only come up with something which rhymed, like a cul de sac in Bearsden or Newton Mearns—to this day upper class suburbs.

This level of enthusiasm from Carlos and Pablo puzzled the students since obviously the family didn't need the money and, coming from Glasgow, they were unsure how to approach the issue of how many pesos the accommodation would cost. And, although the Yanks would be paying, they didn't want to appear cheap. However, being pragmatic Scots, Angela just got to the point and said, "Cuanto cuesta," to which, of course, Carlos promptly replied in Spanish. This made the visitors just a tad nervous.

Things were now getting a wee bit daft and Mary took over and did all of the next round of their communication in English. Fortunately, all four had a finely honed sense of humour and when they replied regarding the pesos, they tried to do this with a Scottish accent. Naturally, now that they had established this important component of their new companions' characters, more drinks were ordered and enjoyed and the arrangement was made for them to visit the possible accommodation the next day. As they travelled back to their temporary accommodation at the uni, they decided that their current situation was meant to be and, as good wee Catholics, they decided that maybe there was a God after all.

A Day of Reckoning

Over breakfast at the University of Havana, in an area called the Common Room, it appeared to the duo that there was something not quite right about it all, and to this end Angela suggested, "let's just put some stuff in a hankie and get out of here." But, in an attempt to appear more with it in regards to both the Cuban culture and the opportunities offered by Carlos and Pablo, Mary declined. Although she was struggling with all the fried stuff that was offered in the Common Room, which appeared to be much more common than even the two Glaswegian East Enders had anticipated. They really—on all of their travels—had never actually eaten chips with breakfast. However, since they were both very fair and non-judgemental, they did concede that they had not experienced chips with everything at breakfast, but had often enjoyed this indulgence at lunch or dinner time.

What intrigued them most about the university was that the dress code, which was almost a uniform, prohibited male and female students from wearing tank tops, flip flops, and short shorts. To Angela and Mary, this was a bit scary in 1977, when most of the western world was doing the opposite in a social sense; hence their discomfort at the level of formality they experienced at their first breakfast in academic Cuba. Anyway, for whatever reason they just didn't feel right in that Common Room, but given that they had actually experienced this Cuban meal, they believed this would serve them well when they set off for their appointment with their potential landlords.

As they moved to the street to hail a fabulous taxi cab, both of these students started to sing with overflowing excitement. Their choice of songs was, of course, Paul McCartney's 'Mull of Kintyre' and Fleetwood Mac's 'Go Your Own Way,' and as the taxicab drew up, they were transported to the next episode of this journey of fairy tale proportions.

Wot? No Darts?

As they got their pesos ready to pay the cool-dude driver who was showing off mercilessly to these young women—whom he had decided were American, with stuff like, "Does anyone live on the ground in New York?" and, "Does everyone have a gun in YOUR country?"—they arrived at the pub. Casa del Mar. And lo and behold there they were: all those chaps sporting casual, quiffed heids and looking rather fetching in the midday sun. Don't forget this was April in Havana.

As Mary and Angela approached the pub, they checked out those in attendance and, not seeing Carlos and Pablo initially, they looked at each other with that flick of the hair, knowingly asking each other the silent question: "Mmm, how many whiskies did we have last night?" Then there they were and then they realised the importance of their question of each other. This was based on the fact that these 'military men' looked somehow absurd with all their locks saturated in a product they knew as 'Brylcreem,' but in their case it just looked like they were on the receiving end of a cold chip pan.

What to do? Well, what to do was that they had to do what was necessary. This involved a completely over the top acknowledgement of last night and acceptance of a midday drink called a Daiquiri. Although the girls had no objection to the introduction of a new product to enhance their nineteen-year-old appetites, Mary managed to whisper to her best mate Angela, "Daiquiri sounds a bit like a disease we might have got in our childhood. You know like your Maw might have said: 'I think she's got a wee touch of Daiquiri, and she'll need a dose of Castor Oil.'" Angela replied knowingly, "Well let's not worry too much. That Castor Oil seemed to fix most of our ailments when we were wee. How about we just enjoy it and stop behaving like Presbyterians."

The four of them smiled indulgently, stood up for the longest time and then settled into what was typical of any opposite sex lunch time socialising in a pub. It was a bit tentative at first—not like the night before with the help of the whisky—but then they settled down and a more formal situation emerged. Well, if Mary and Angela were about to secure decent accommodation, there had to be a level of formality. Still, the more they conversed, albeit within certain strictures of the boys' and girls' English language skills, the more Mary fancied Carlos, but Pablo seemed to do nothing much for Angela. This was to become a bit of an issue over time. They agreed that one drink was enough and that they should get themselves over to the casa to meet their landlady and landlord: Antonietta and Adolpho.

So essentially it was important to talk of the people who might be very involved in their lives during the next few years. They named them A2 (squared) affectionately and indeed they used this always when necessary to discuss them. They did not actually find out their hosts' surname, which was Almada, until later that day, so they endeavoured to try A3 (treble), but that just didn't have the same ring to it so they maintained A-squared.

Later when they got to know A-squared they decided to check what these names represented: Antonietta (invaluable) and Adolpho (noble wolf) respectively, and Almada, which of course was Adolpho's family name.

It meant powerful and complete. You are good intellectually and require several outlets for your energies. You are not a builder but a planner, and you want others to carry out your plans. You are bold, independent, inquisitive and interested in research. You know what you want and why you want it.

You are seeking freedom and opportunities to enjoy life; to make love, to go places and to do things. You are very adventurous and willing to take risks to achieve your objectives. New ways and new experiences can't satisfy your restless nature. One adventure leads you to another. You are honest and fair, because you know that this is the only way to receive justice and honesty from other people. But your personal growth is vital for you, and it is difficult to be tied down by rules and obligations. Your restless spirit might best be controlled by choosing the field of work that meets your demand for action and adventure.

Almada is also a city on the banks of the River Tagus with a remarkable history of foment between Christianity and Islam, but has been, for a long time, a city of Portugal with a population of 100,000.

Naturally, Mary and Angela sought information regarding the maiden name of Antonietta. It transpired that her name was Aborachi Beje—and guess what? It was a Jewish name. Antonietta's origins were from the region near Salamanca in Spain called Bejer. So…if she was of Jewish origin, in keeping with Jewish culture, the boys of the family Almada were deemed to be Jewish too. If the adventurers thought their heritage was interesting—all those hordes from Scandinavia, etc—this denouement was by far much more intriguing. However, Antonietta did not have a lavish account of her propensities.

There was something a wee bit spooky about the fact that these two people had met and married with the letter A in both of their first and second names. When this was raised to Carlos and Pablo, they shrugged and, whilst agreeing it was a bit unusual, they suggested they rather liked the idea and hoped they might be lucky enough to find partners who at least shared one starting initial. Again, with a swish of their hair, Mary and Angela signalled A for Angela and Almada. The plot thickens….

Casa and Beyond

It was now past two pm and seemed the right time to get on their way to the House of Almada. The duo kept trying to say the names of their hosts —but boy did they struggle to get the names swiftly off their tongues. Adolpho Almada and Antonietta Aborachi Beher Almada.

The address of their future home was 226 Paseo del Prado, which was amazingly close to the Maritime Promenade, The Malecon, and extremely sought after. Everybody who was somebody had seen it on the telly or in their dreams.

Although it was called a casa (which in the girls' world meant a house as opposed to a flat), the boys' family home was indeed an apartment, but more like the Dakota building where John Lennon was assassinated (not that they knew that in 1977). But of course ultimately they could reflect on this.

Carlos and Pablo were striding ahead of Mary and Angela, checking every once in a step or two that they were still behind. Well, indeed they were because they genuinely believed that they had scored in this accommodation and indeed they were not disappointed.

As they approached the entrance to this magnificent edifice, Carlos and Pablo dashed to the gracious front door—which was a relic of an era certainly not of the current Communist stronghold. In fact, as Mary and Angela teetered up the pathway their locks swung in unison and they both understood their rather anguished exchange to be one of foreboding. This was based on the fact that in all of their travels they had not encountered such opulence and wondered how they would fare. It was usual for them to be humbled by much and this was due to their common-sense rearing in working-class Glasgow. On the other hand, if they were to impress and be accepted as suitable for lodgings in such obviously affluent conditions, they would be obliged not to exhibit any surprise or gaffes when alluding to their own humble beginnings. There was nothing political about this, but Mary and Angela later confirmed that they felt some kind of resentment which was later reflected in their future careers. For now though they were both happy to share their strategies for acceptance.

Seconds after arrival, they were greeted profusely and escorted to a very comfortable but classy front room in old parlance and invited to a pre-prandial Scotch of Johnny Walker Red—obviously their predilection had been indicated yesterday by the boys to the landlady and landlord.

Antonietta was attired in a very louche pant suit which was predominantly of a lazy peach hue. Yes, pant suit, as was very popular in the West at that time. Where had she acquired such a non-Cuban style? Whereas Alphonso was dressed in a much more formal collar and tie with flared trousers, which was not a good look for the girls. Fortunately, due to their social training they were able to keep their incredulity to themselves for later hilarity.

Initially, they all sat around a table where coffee was served and observed all the decorum, except that the girls were hanging for a deep fried Mars bar—a Glasgow delicacy. The boys had advised that Adolpho was currently an Army General in the Cuban Armed Forces. Although Mary and Angela didn't know this then, the assistance from the Soviet Government's military from 1966 until the late 1980s enabled Cuba to upgrade its military capabilities to be number one in Latin America and allowed them to project power abroad. The first Cuban military mission in Africa was established in Ghana in 1961, but more importantly the Cuban intervention in Angola from 1975 to 1989 was currently the situation for Adolpho, who was on leave for a couple of weeks; hence he was around the discussion table regarding the tenants. So, a military family was the reality for the peace-loving Scottish lassies, which did engender a few moments of discomfort since the notion of the military in the UK in 1977 was confined to the 'The Troubles,' which were all about Northern Ireland and the UK. While this was a bloody conflict primarily about sectarianism, it was somehow different from 'foreign' stuff.

It was therefore difficult for the girls to establish what Antonietta had done for her years of marriage to Adolpho. However, given the times in Cuba, it was possible that she had not been deemed to have achieved very much, save being a good, solid wife and mother with only one interest outside the home which was, funnily enough, the sport of basketball. Indeed, she was the secretary of the local club and as such she had access to the team and those young men who aspired to become 'great' in this game which attracted and ensnared the American players to Cuba during this period. There had inevitably been much speculation regarding this very beautiful woman and the contradiction in her life pursuits.

Due to his high ranking military position Alphonso earned a decent salary; but it did puzzle Mary in particular—who was always a wee bit cynical about many things—that even on a salary like the General's she pondered his ability to buy the casa, which really was luxurious, straight out of Beverly Hills and more.

Whilst worrying about a deep fried Mars bar, all of a sudden a young man appeared at the doorway from the luxurious dining room and beckoned everyone to the dining table, which was almost better than a GPlan of its time. Out came lovely sweet white wine and a serious red. This young man was also called Carlos and they were greeted with a table which could have outsmarted a similar table in Bearsden in Glasgow. This new Carlos certainly confirmed the Cuban Communist ideology of social equality in every way, since he had a very humble presence in complete contrast to the Carlos and Pablo the girls had come to know.

Again, Mary—who could not really have been very savvy about these things—was puzzled about the largesse of the delights of the dining fare. The delights included those made with pork, chicken, rice, beans, tomatoes and lettuce. Hot spices are rarely used in Cuban cooking but fried (pollo frito) or grilled (polloassado) chicken and grilled pork were more typical at the time in Cuba. Beef and seafood were rarely prepared except for lobster (which became so popular they ran the risk of becoming endangered in Cuba. Rabbit (conejo) when available was also enjoyed.

As they tucked into the more posh dishes with great zest, Angela did not appear to notice anything untoward but Mary, the detective, did have a few puzzled thoughts. She could not understand that Angela was not at least curious because at uni they had been subjected by and large to rice, rice and more rice.

Never mind all that, they thought surreptitiously, let's smile and be gracious. Fortunately, A-squared had good English language skills and had no idea really of their Glasgow accent and so the 'interview' went swimmingly. They finished their drinks and were given a tour of the mansion and their separate bedrooms with easy access to the lavish bathroom they were to share, and the view was amazing considering the mansion was in the heart of Havana! This view was of a small orchard with an abundance of citrus fruits as well as grapes, mangoes and many other fruitful indulgences. Albeit at this stage in their lives, Mary and Angela had not yet experienced the luxury of the mango.

No price had yet been negotiated, but Mary had rehearsed how to engage in this sensitivity and when they got to dessert (mango nectar) Mary raised the issue, making the assumption that money was the last thing rich people discussed. However, Antonietta was articulate in the pricing and a deal was reached within minutes and a three-year contract signed. This was later sent to Guantanamo and the deal was done. Of course, this would be paid by the American authorities, which challenged A-squared for a minute, but the conclusion was that this would be a much more reliable financial deal, making the young woman feel a tad offended. "Onwards and upwards," they declared, with a swing of the locks.

Exiting Cuba...

As the girls wound their way back to the uni they decided they would have a Scotch and soda in what was now their local. The taxi driver had the same kind characteristics as all of their taxi drivers to date, and which they would enjoy for a while to come—there being no opportunity to achieve a deep fried Mars bar! No Uber in those days.

As they settled in their now favourite spot in the bar, Mary became aware of the newly introduced Carlos, who slowly leaned over and said, "Hello." He went on to say, whilst focused on Mary, that he had seen them a few times in the bar and was sooo thrilled that in his recent chats with the original Carlos he was advised of Mary and Angela, and now hoped that he could join them for a bit. The girls said, "Of course," and this was the beginning of a relationship between him and Mary.

Unfortunately, Mary was rather enchanted by Carlos of the Casa and became a bit anxious and wondered how it would all turn out.

However, in the meantime, the more they chatted, the more his accent seemed to change and Mary dug a bit deeper and realised there was an underlying Glasgow accent which was overwhelmed from time to time by an Australian one. At this stage (still in the pub) Mary requested they call him CarlosO, so as to not confuse him with Carlos, which would run the risk of gossip re: the wrong one. He also took the opportunity to confess that his real name was Hamish, which resulted in a hugely shared laugh out loud. There was a lot to come.

And so the lives of Mary and Angela continued as things do for students no matter what culture. On top of the pressures of learning, they settled quickly into their casa of luxury about which they could not stop sharing their totally unexpected adventures.

Inevitably of course, their relationships with the brothers Carlos and Pablo developed more each day, in particular that of Carlos and Mary. However, Mary was not aware that CarlosA also fancied her big time but Angela—who did not fancy either of the boys—was very aware of what was going on. In due course Carlos declared his hand in his pursuit of Mary, which was reciprocated big time so that dye was cast and Carlos accepted this outcome.

What followed was likely only to be in a story but it was for real in their continuing story which was absolutely true. What happened? Pablo and Angela fell in love even more passionately than their counterparts and the four friends enjoyed six months of sharing and caring (Carlos from Australia got work for this time in Havana); but good things often come to an end and in this case it was all about their futures. With the permission of his parents, the landlord and lady gave their blessing to Carlos and Mary who married within a month, as did Pablo and Angela. Two weddings (and approved by Carlos and Pablo's parents) were organised as a serious event in the social circles of the 'A' family, as well as being representative of the big mix of cultures. Of course, the weddings were Catholic and were performed in the local cathedral.

The event was captured by the local newspaper and Mary and Angela were sooo beautiful, especially given the speed with which they had to organise it all. The reception had a couple of local Cuban music bands and the grub was even more complex than the girls had devoured to date. They inherited a couple of beautiful bedrooms in the mansion and for the next few weeks, until the boys had to decide what was next, the debates continued in the magnificent comfort of the casa.

However the big issues of their outside of Cuba destinations had not yet been resolved. For example, Angola and Mozambique were the obvious temporary locations for Carlos and Mary since he had followed his father's footsteps and would be required to spend his future with that of Cuba. His military position was Colonel, so that decision was very limited for Mary. But Angola it became.

CarlosO was at that time a senior marketing manager of a major Florida supermarket chain.

The girls had a contemporary knowledge of Eastern Europe after working while inter-railing for the best part of a year in several countries, such as in farms and vineyards in Croatia, Romania and Bulgaria; but their real knowledge was of African states, such as Angola or Mozambique, and Cuba, due to their relationship with Cuba during the time they found themselves indeed in Cuba. Cuba was involved in the future of Angola (ex-Portuguese colony.). At this particular period, Cuba was not seriously involved with the scenario of Mozambique. So, there was an inevitability about Mary's immediate future and that was to go onward to Angola.

At this time Angela had accepted her fate, which was to be ensconced in Florida, which excited her rather than producing any foreboding.

Therefore, within two or three weeks, the plans were developed, but the issue of transport to both destinations was a big issue. The transport to Angola was plentiful, but only for the troops, and the transport to Florida was also limited by several criteria, so the Florida 'transfer' was also limited to those who had an independent business record. What to do?

Interestingly, a relative of CarlosA—a very successful business achiever in the major tourism industry in Miami—had recently arrived in Cuba to capitalise on Cuba's current rise in the areas in which he was involved and successful. Allen (currently from Australia) was invited to dinner with the foursome and naturally the transport issue was raised. Allen immediately divulged that he had his own aircraft and, for a small fee, he would be happy to accommodate their needs, and so the dye was cast. His plane could seat six people, and it was agreed that CarlosA and Angela would be flown to Florida and after Allen's return to Cuba the flight to Luanda, Angola's capital, was undertaken.

Mary and Angela could not believe how everything had fallen into place vis-à-vis their needs and road to happiness. Whilst the 'Cuban' side of things were so well addressed by Allen Constantino —'Constant Pleasure' in Sydney, Australia—he established himself and with his business acumen in Havana and its environs. His success had been confirmed earlier in Florida—subsequently in Australia, but maintaining his success in Florida.

This scenario was easily one of the most exciting components of their young lives and was now upon them and Angela's next life component happened easily and soon. She and Carlos left like two children on their first flight. Allen's aircraft seemed like first class all the way (he had hired an assistant), with first class food and wine and reading material —naturally related to business success. Indeed, Florida offered the opportunity Angela had longed for, and within a three month period, with the assistance of Allen and Carlos, her dream vegetarian haggis restaurant took off within the first three months of arrival in Miami. It was called 'Happy Haggis,' and she and Carlos had the best of times, and their future included three wee ones who, as they grew, managed to mimic their Mum's Glasgow accent, which was a great attraction to Angela's market due to the Scottish tourists, of whom there were many. She also managed to get to Scotland a couple of times per annum and her Scottish family and pals were still shaking their heads at her success!

It was of course more difficult to achieve entry to Angola for Mary, even though she was the wife of the Colonel. However, in due course she obtained permission provided she donated a serious sum of money prior to entry and, although she was indignant about the whole process, this indignation gave way to excitement and potential.

The touchdown city for them was the capital of Angola, Luanda, whose population in the 1970s was 60,000. Out of her own interest, Mary established that Glasgow at that time had 1.7 million and she kind of felt pleased about that. Nevertheless, Luanda it was, and it was a given that her husband would be gainfully employed in the Cuban barracks (she was also resident in the barracks with him). He was therefore 'away' a lot of the time ensuring that the MPLA (Communist-aligned People's Movement for the Liberation of Angola) was progressing. This movement was directly against other 'unions,' and the most important opposition for Cuban involvement was the National Liberation Front of Angola (FNLA), which was ideologically pro-Western, resulting in the independence of Angola from the Portuguese.

Mary therefore had to be as innovative as possible in a very strange environment—even more so than her arrival in complex Cuba, but she was a woman of strength and innovation. This strength and innovation resulted in her establishment of a dog shelter for abused dogs and those without a home. Her premises were enabled by a disused bakery which had retained its encouraging emissions. She was readily subsidised by the local authority who gained respect in these horrendous war times in the capital. In other words, Mary's initiative rendered a skerrick of respectful culture in war-torn Luanda.

Mary's success was based somewhat on her family's caring and sharing world, especially when it came to all the unpleasant happenings relative to dog welfare. She therefore inherited that culture and was now able to formalise those values. Lucky for her, her husband was with her all the way and conceded that dog welfare was not taken as a big enough issue in contemporary Cuba and indeed contemporary Angola. He understood.

It took about two weeks for Mary to set things up, which included accommodation for her patient's needs. She managed subtle advertising in a specific area of the city and the first day she was open she smiled continuously for a couple of hours and then —voilà! The door opened and a young woman entered with a rather dishevelled wee dog.

Through her smiles, Mary became aware that, as opposed to announcing the plight of the dog which was accompanying the first 'client,' they both looked at each other for a text book smile and all was revealed. The 'client' was one of the friends she had made during her sortie into Lithuania a couple of years previously. Mary had been fascinated by Debra because she had hailed from Arizona, which had intrigued Mary at the time. While in Lithuania they had become very, very, close in every way. Their notion of absurdity in the premises was their common denominator, which was confirmed as they continued to look at each other without actually speaking. Both were obviously reflecting on their relationship in Lithuania, with Mary desperately seeking the reason why Debra was currently in an unsafe part of the world. This was answered in due course by Debra's account of a woman who had embarked on the European world—just like Mary and Debra. But her culture was African, particularly of Western South Africa, who had a huge component of history in Angola.: da! da!

The friend Helen had enjoyed Debra, who was now ensconced in Angola for a bit—no great compulsion—but assisted by Mary and Helen to investigate the politics currently putting Angola at terrible risks. And many people whom Mary and Debra encountered along the way reflected on the fact that Portugal had been definitively a colonial power for a long period of time. *Quelle surprise*! In due course it emerged that Helen was a South African spy. This emergence was absolutely fascinating for Mary and Debra and they enjoyed Helen's 'uncovering' of so much information about current political Angola which was, in a crazy way, exciting.

This led Mary to investigate further and specifically about the contemporary culture of Portugal. This investigation was based on her increasing thoughts of a future which would include Debra and be in Europe. At this stage, it appeared that Debra had no social commitments across the board, which of course offered some solace for Mary who was now on a mission. This was not the denouement Mary had envisaged, but as the days moved on and since she didn't see much of her soldier man, she decided that after all 'her woman' Debra was more relevant and wonderful and fulfilled and was all that she had envisaged in a serious partnership that she had not experienced to date avec her soldier husband.

She and Debra talked and talked, and at this stage in history most nationalities were able to choose a European country in which to sell their labour or perhaps to migrate. They were so excited and, as they knew the little adage, 'Once the decision is made, the rest is easy,' they deemed themselves to be home and dry.

After about fifteen minutes deliberation, the die was cast and Denmark it was! No doubt they would thrive in the dog world and no doubt that the area of Copenhagen Mermaid would make a good start! They decided to leave Angola as soon as possible, which was within two weeks and they quickly assembled their CVs and agreed that their experiences would serve them well in such a very complicated world. Mary conceded that she would miss Cuba more than she had anticipated.

The irony of everything was concluded when the soldier announced he had had a second encounter with a soldier who had been in his life for quite a while in Cuba, and Mary's confession fell on sort of appreciated ears. He was now free (freed) to follow his heart as Mary pursued hers. Debra was overjoyed at this unbelievable progression, which was almost a dream come true.

Sensibly, they chose to keep quiet about their plans, particularly with regard to family, with the exception of the lovely, and now Floridian, Angela and her wonderful husband. Interestingly, almost out of the blue, Angela informed them of her Haggis success, attaching the cute poem:

> *Oh Haggis, wee haggis*
> *Where have ye been*
> *Since the turn of the century*
> *When times were lean*

Running round hills like a dog
After its tail
Ye ran through the snow, rain and the hail
Oh, Haggis, ma wee haggis
Yer a mysterious thing
From over the glen I can
Hear yer clan sing
And when bagpipes are wailing
Their sad lament
I swear I can see ye all shrivelled and bent
Oh, Haggis, wee haggis, yer
An endangered breed,
Yer just like the Scots in the
Books that we read
They chased the Sassenachs
With remarkable speed
The proud Lion Rampant o'er their heeds
Oh Haggis, wee haggis yer a
National feature
Yer as famous as Nessy that
Mythical creature
Amin Scottish heather
Blooming purple and white
Folks search for ye till the
Wee sma' hoors of the night
Oh, Haggis, dear haggis, may
Ye never be found

With one leg shorter ye'll still'
Cover the ground.
Just like the Scots for yer
Freedom, ye'll fight
And you'll remain a legend for ever
In your own right
Catriona Ferrie

This wee poem excited Mary so much and she could not wait to hear of the success of 'Happy Haggis' Angela in Florida

The Plain Child was no longer plain in any possible way as she and her wonderful partner Debra mounted their economy seating on their long journey from troubled Angola to the excitement of 'the place to be' in this seventies world, which was Copenhagen.

The Plain Child's adventures for the next decade are the content of the next episode of their three lives:

The Plain Child Soars…

Author Notes

[1] Interestingly, President William McKinley (assassinated in 1901) stated that 'Cuba ought to be free and independent, and the government should be turned over to the Cuban people.' Although this was not supported by all, the quote does demonstrate rather clearly that the USA and Cuba did not always view each other as enemies. This is based on the fact that Cuban politics were not of the Communist variety at that time and pre-dates Fidel Castro and the Cuban Revolution.

Photos

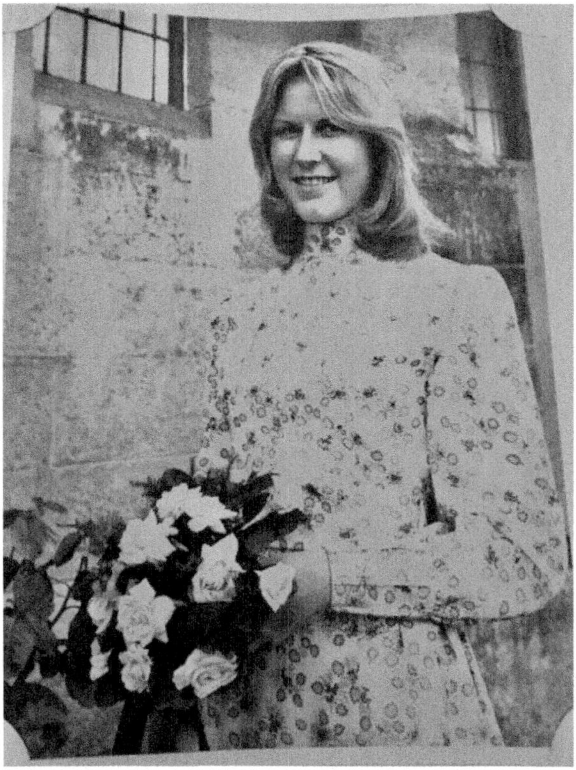

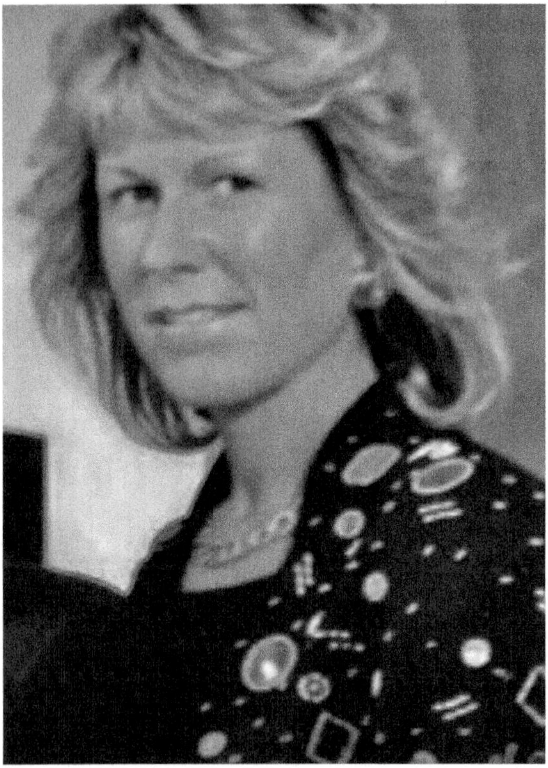

About the Author

Mattie (Martha) was born in the East End of Glasgow and matured there. She revels in the place and the historical time in which she grew up - 1960s.

Employment was taken for granted and believed 'if you get fed up with job number one, just cross the road and get a better one'.

With a couple of pals she went off to Canada for a couple of years which confirmed a life she had already enjoyed. Her Canadian experience was a wee bit too nice for her and she went back to Glasgow with the proverbial 'bells on'.

In due course, she married her friend of yesteryear and off they went with their three children to South Africa in 1975; just at the beginning-of-the-end of Apartheid - great times!

Husband Jack (Scottish Accountant) was offered a position with huge company in Toronto which lasted for about five years and then voila!! In 1984 Australia beckoned. The rest is all about positivity. Mattie chose to get a degree at the University where she worked for a time. Scribe to many organisations (including the State Parliament) and ultimately, her local university where she entered the world of academia; ensuring she qualified in the teaching arena and is still in that place.Ultimately she achieved an Honours and a Masters degree.

Her previous book was about the experiences of Scottish children evacuees during World War Two.

She concedes that 'The Plain Child' could not be further from the Evacuation stories but she has enjoyed the adventures emanating from her with The Plain Child travels along with her sister's bestie.

Printed in Great Britain
by Amazon